I0558080

Room at the Inn

Activities K-8

Rose-Volpini Hand

and

Peter Tassi

This book belongs to:

_____

TREASURES

You probably have Treasures in your life. Things you value a great deal, and take pride in owning. Treasures always make you feel good because of the good memories they bring to mind. Treasures are important to have and take care of.

Think about 3 Treasures that you have. Write about each one. Share your work with the class.

LOOK AT THESE TWO PICTURES

Both the human and the trees need things to grow.
Using a chart, list all the things they need to live
and grow.

Tree	Human

HELPING HEARTS

Whenever we help others we get something good from it. If we help someone, we give them a part of ourselves. We become helping hearts. It's very important that we always leave room in our hearts for others. If we do this, then others will have room for us.

In each heart write the name of someone you have room for. Make more hearts if you need to.

Find the words in this word puzzle. Print them in the spaces below.

```
E B R E A D O V E T S
G I V I N G L O V E P
A L I V E S K E N D A
S A V E L O R D T Y N
E J E S U S S O N S T
T C R O S S B R O Y L
```

1. _____ 2. _____ 3. _____ 4. _____ 5. _____
6. _____ 7. _____ 8. _____ 9. _____ 10. _____

CODE

A	B	C	D	E	F	G	H	I	J	K	L	M	N	O	P	Q	R	S	T	U	V	W	X	Y	Z
14	13	16	19	2	1	20	15	22	4	23	18	5	7	9	10	6	24	8	15	16	12	17	21	3	11

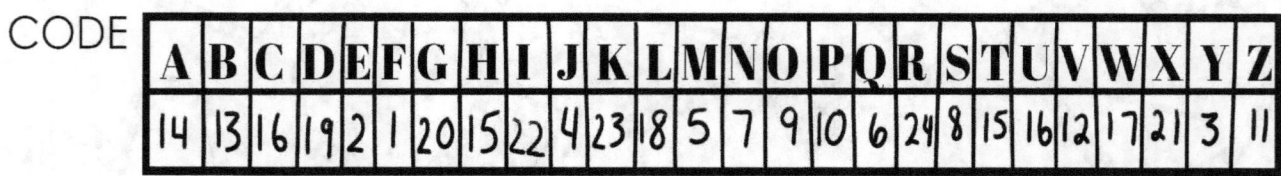

3   9   26   14 24 2   14   8 10 2 16 22 14 18

16 15 22 18 19   9   1   20 9 19

Above is a picture of a fishing boat in a storm. Jesus calmed the storm and brought peace to the apostles who were on the boat. Jesus brings us peace everyday of our lives. How do you think he does this?

_____

_____

_____

_____

_____

ALL LIFE COMES FROM GOD

Here are some of the things that belong to God's family. Name each one and color it in.

1

2

3

4

5

6

7

8

Make a picture of something that belongs to God's family.

Jesus left us some important symbols to help us remember Him. Around the circle are the words for the symbols below. Draw a picture inside the circle of Jesus.

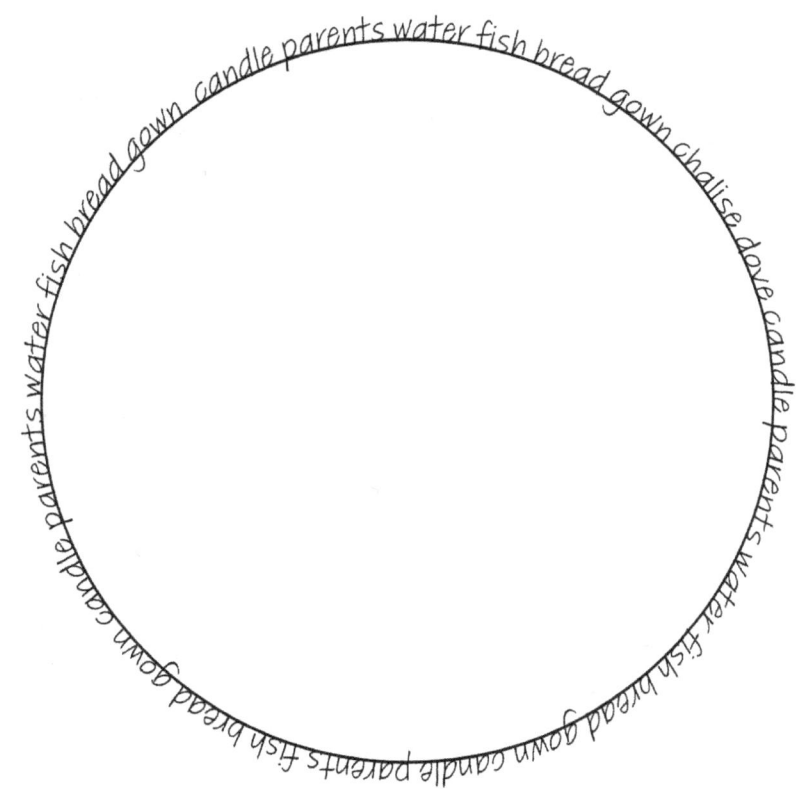

candle parents water fish bread gown chalise dove candle parents water fish bread gown parents fish bread gown candle parents water fish bread gown candle parents water fish bread gown candle parents

Write the words on the lines below the symbols.

Jesus had a lot of friends because he knew how to share with others.

When we share our things, our talents, and our lives with others, we are acting like Jesus.

Other people act like Jesus when they share their lives with us.

Write down how these people listed below share with us.

Teacher_____
_____
_____
_____

Mom and Dad_____
_____
_____
_____

Grandma and Grandpa_____
_____
_____
_____

We can see in all the seasons that things change. Whatever dies in Fall and winter comes back to life in Spring.

Fall

Winter

Spring

Summer

Fill in this chart with words and pictures that tell what happens in each season.

Fall	Winter
Spring	Summer

DEAR GOD; THIS IS MY THANK YOU PICTURE TO YOU. YOUR CHILD,

_____

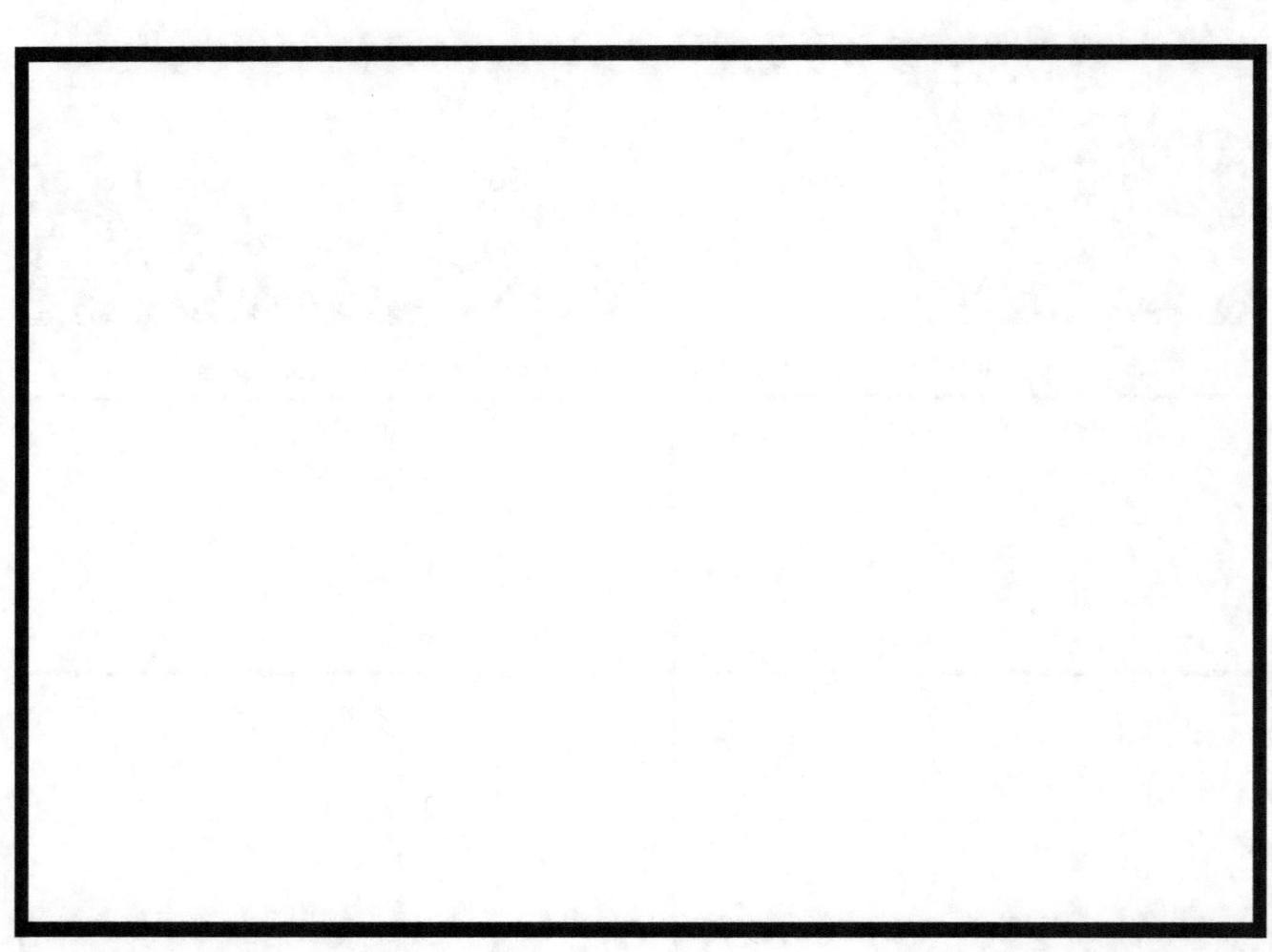

Write your answers in the shapes!

How old were you when you were baptized?

Who baptized Jesus?

What church were you baptized in?

What river was Jesus baptized in?

Read Matthew 3:13-17

Now that you are baptized, what two families do you belong to?

Who was at your baptism?

How old was Jesus when he was baptized?

Read these scriptures, and discover how Jesus and Paul were able to change people.

Matthew 9:10-13

Luke 13:10-13

John 8:2-11

Acts 20:7-12

Acts 16:25-34

Write a short paragraph on how you can be like Jesus and Paul at home and at school.

Once you have let a lot of people into your heart you will begin to give and recieve lots of treasures. Remember, every good deed is a treasure. Just like a beautiful diamond or precious pearl.

Below are some diamonds. They are the treasures you give to others, and treasures others give to you.

Fill in each treasure with a good deed.

Treasures I give   Treasures I receive

Below is a circle, divided into 4 sections. In each section write the name of a friend and what

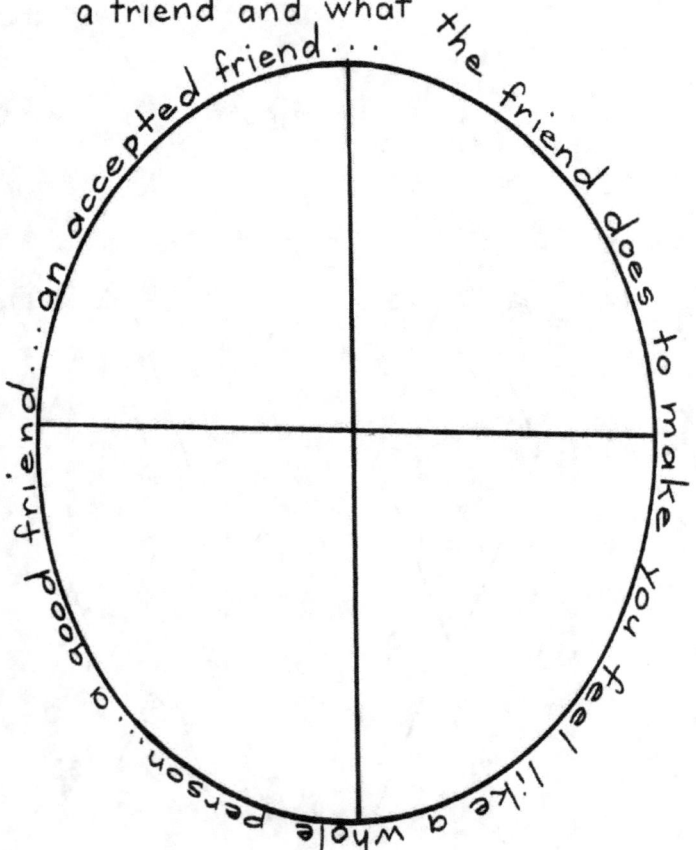

the friend does to make you feel like a whole person... a good friend... an accepted friend...

In each section write the name of a friend, and what you have done to make your friendship better.

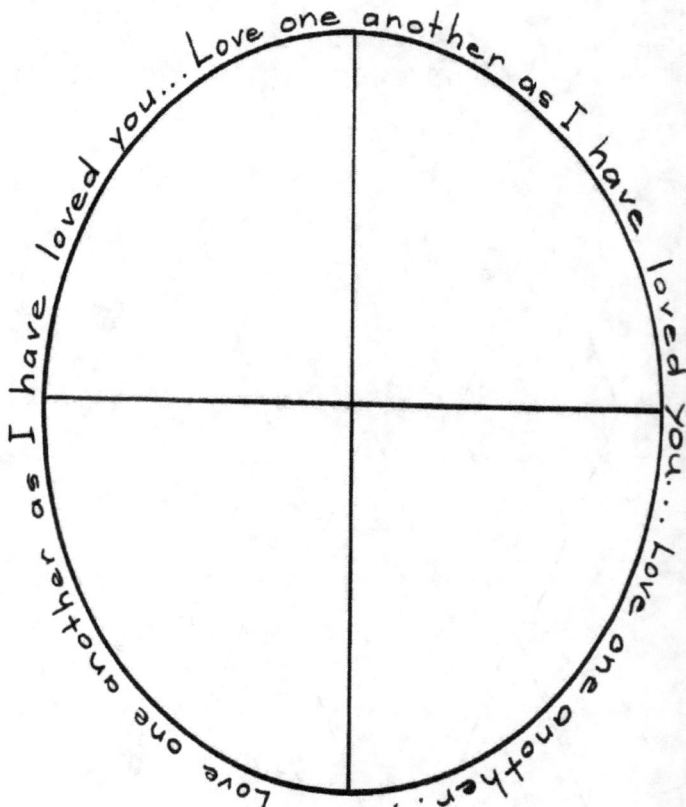

Love one another as I have loved you... Love one another... Love one another as I have loved you...

Read this section from Corinthians I and II.

Paul travelled to many places including Corinth. During his visits he spoke of God's love and encouraged the people to be more like Jesus.
After returning home, Paul would write letters to the people in different parts of the world. Paul would ask them how they were and he would talk to them about Jesus. He also emphasized what Jesus expected of them.

Read one of Paul's letters and list some of the things Paul mentioned.

Put yourself in Paul's place.
   * You have just returned home from a journey.
   * You are writing to encourage the people to be all the things Jesus wants them to be.
   * What would you tell them?

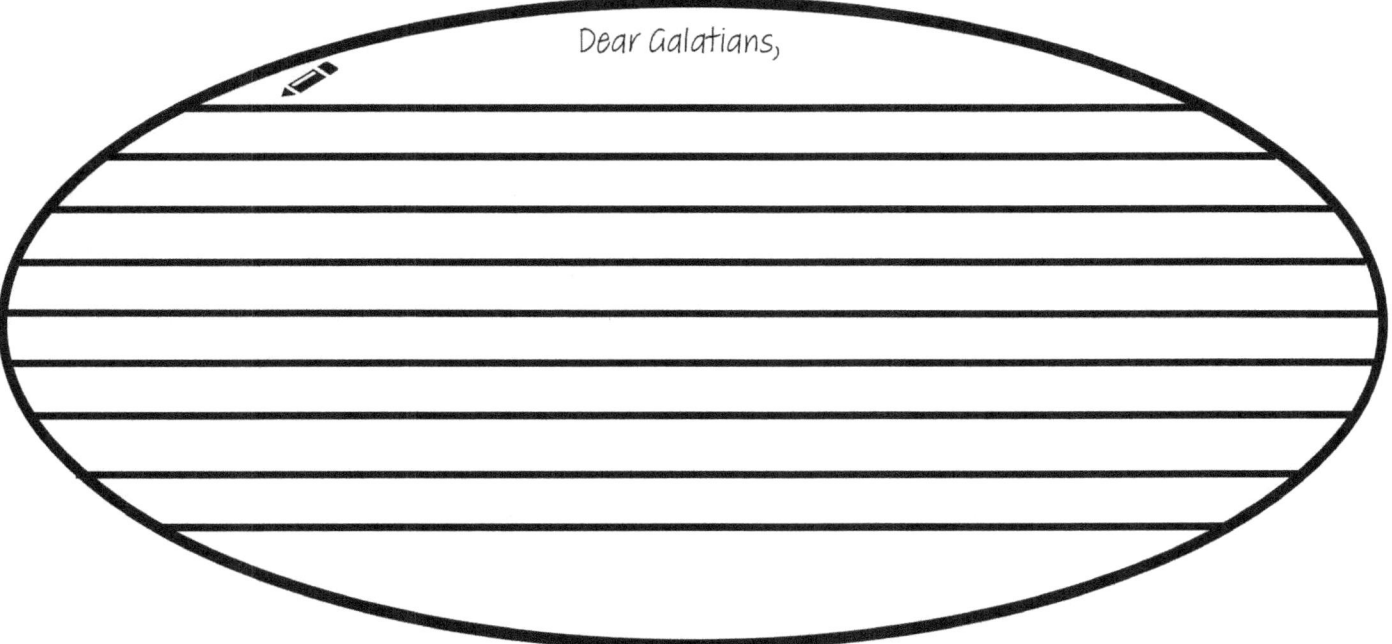

Dear Galatians,

Talking it Out

Jesus wants us to talk to Him, and tell Him what we are thinking. Sometimes problems bother us and makes us think bad thoughts about others.

Jesus wants us to talk to Him about these problems so that He can help us.

Quietly, let's think about things that bother us and tell Jesus about them.

...in the house...
...at supper...
...at bedtime....
...lining up....
at recess time...
...in the yard...
...in your room..

Write a letter to Jesus telling Him about something thats a problem for you.

Dear Jesus,

_____

_____

_____

_____

_____

_____

_____

_____

How do your parents, friends, teachers, care for you when you are sick, sad, lonely, troubled, afraid, and need help?

Sick_____

_____

_____

Sad_____

_____

_____

Lonely_____

_____

_____

Troubled_____

_____

_____

Afraid_____

_____

_____

Need help_____

_____

_____

Jesus is always here with us. He is our Best Friend.

Think of times when you need Jesus to help you. Tell the class about those times.

At home_____
_____
_____
_____

At school_____
_____
_____
_____

At play_____
_____
_____
_____

Jesus loves us. Each of us has a special gift or talent. God gave us this talent so that we can serve Him in a special way.

Think about each person in the room. Write the name of each student, and one talent that you think each student has. If you need extra space use a blank piece of paper to add more.

Your teacher will fill in a note to you at the bottom.

Name   Gift

_____   _____

_____   _____

_____   _____

_____   _____

_____   _____

_____   _____

Teacher: My student_____has a special gift. The gift is

_____

_____.

Sometimes we do things that hurt Jesus,
but he forgives us when we say we're sorry. Jesus wants us
to forgive each other.

Tell Jesus who you have forgiven.

Dear Jesus,
_____
_____
_____
_____

_____
_____
_____
_____ your friend,
_____

Dear Jesus,
_____
_____
_____
_____
_____

your friend,
_____

Draw a time when Jesus cared for you when you were lonely.

Jesus showed how much he loved others by caring for them.

Tell us how Jesus showed these people he cared for them.

Sick People_____

_____

Hungry people_____

_____

Lonely people_____

_____

Poor people_____

_____

Tell us when you are a good friend to someone.

We're good friends when we act like JESUS

1. Listen to a friend who has a problem._____
_____
_____

2. Help someone finish school work._____
_____
_____

3. Share my things with someone. _____
_____
_____

4. Play with someone I don't like. _____
_____
_____
_____

Pen Pal

If you had a pen pal in another country, and you wanted to invite them to your house for the summer, what would you write to welcome them and make them feel welcome.

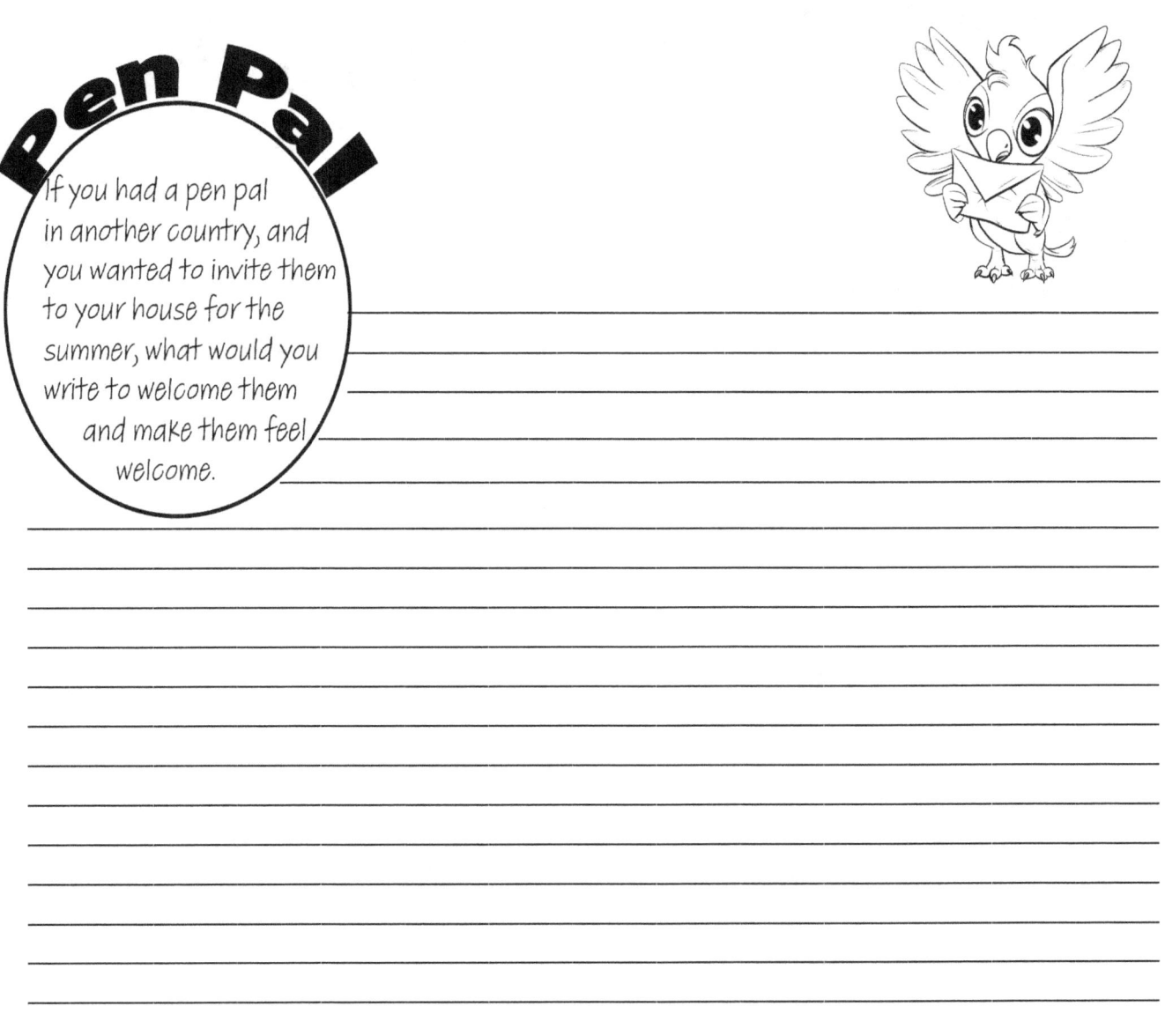

WE ALL BELONG TO GOD

Water is a wonderful gift from God. God used water in a special way. He filled rivers, lakes, oceans, streams, and seas with life.
We use water for many things. It is very important to us, and helps keep us alive.

Write some of the ways we use water.

_____

_____

_____

_____

_____

_____

_____

_____

_____

_____

_____

_____

_____

ABOVE ARE FOOTPRINTS MADE BY JESUS.

Make your footprints beside Jesus'.
Beside each footprint, write a quality that
you need to walk and work with Jesus.

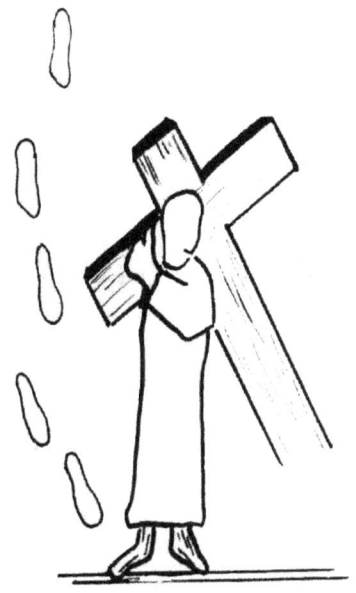

GAS IS MADE UP OF COMPOUNDS SUCH AS, KNOWLEDGE,

You're going on a long trip so you have to "GAS UP." The gas represents things you need in life to go on the journey. As you travel along, you will need to make decisions and make the right choices. Write down at each turn, the names of people who will help you.

FILL IN THINGS THIS CITY NEEDS

Examples: Buildings, signs, etc.

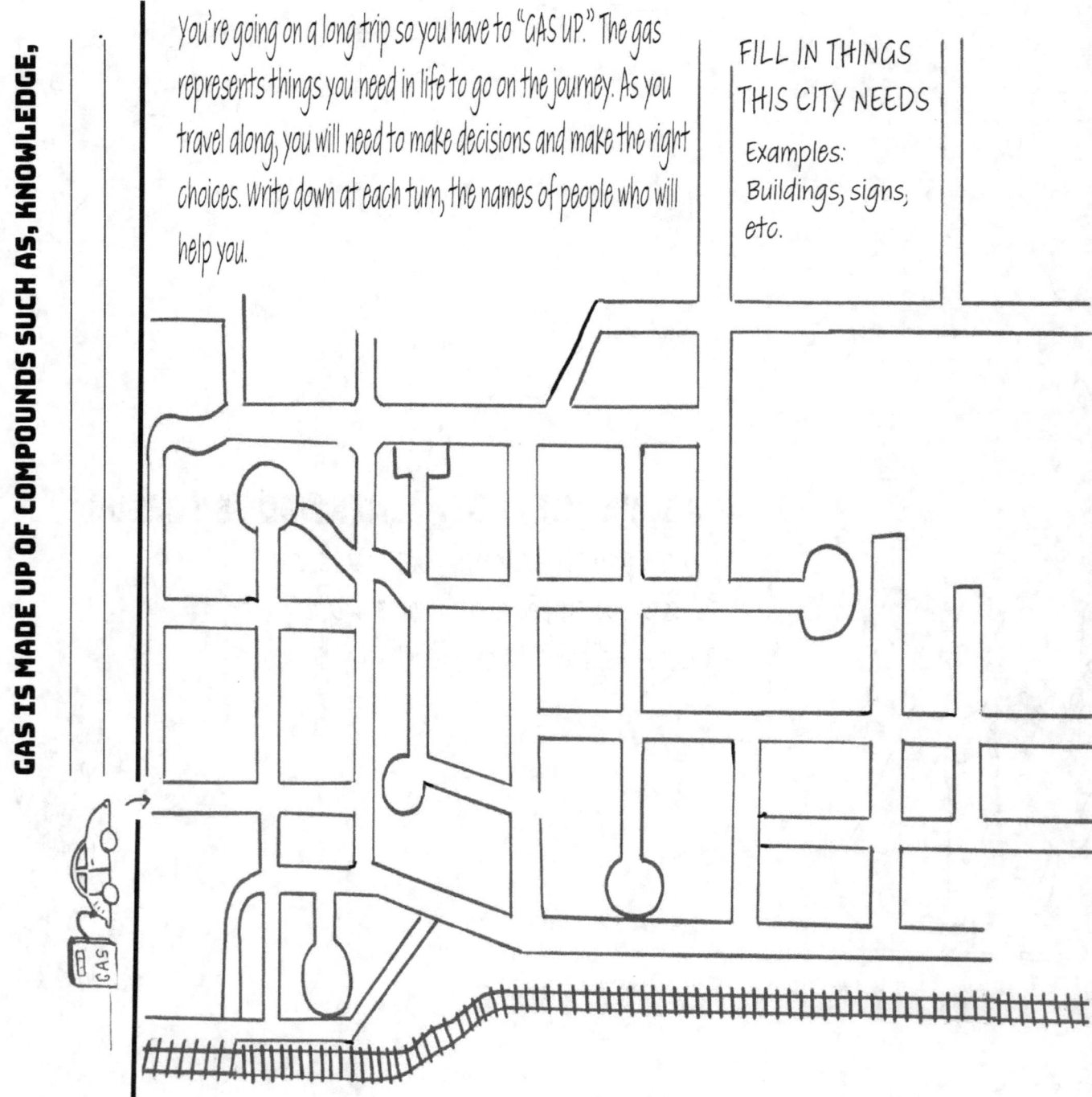

DID SOMEONE OR SOMETHING YOU LOVED DIE, LIKE A PET, PERSON, OR EVEN A PLANT YOU LIKED?

When things or people we love die, we feel very sad and lonely. When Jesus died, his mother and his friends felt very lonely, very sad, and very afraid. Jesus only died for a little while. Jesus rose from the dead to give us a new life. Now, when anyone or anything dies, we can feel happy knowing that they are with God. Now we know that they are alive again with Jesus. Now we can be happy.

Write a story telling how you felt when someone or something you loved died. Tell how you feel now that you know they are alive again in heaven with Jesus.

_____

_____

_____

_____

_____

_____

_____

_____

_____

_____

_____

_____

CELEBRATE A SPECIAL STAR

Can you think of some people you have seen on T.V. who shared something with others? Do you know anyone who shares with others? Colour a star for each person you know who shares with others, and write that person's name under the star.

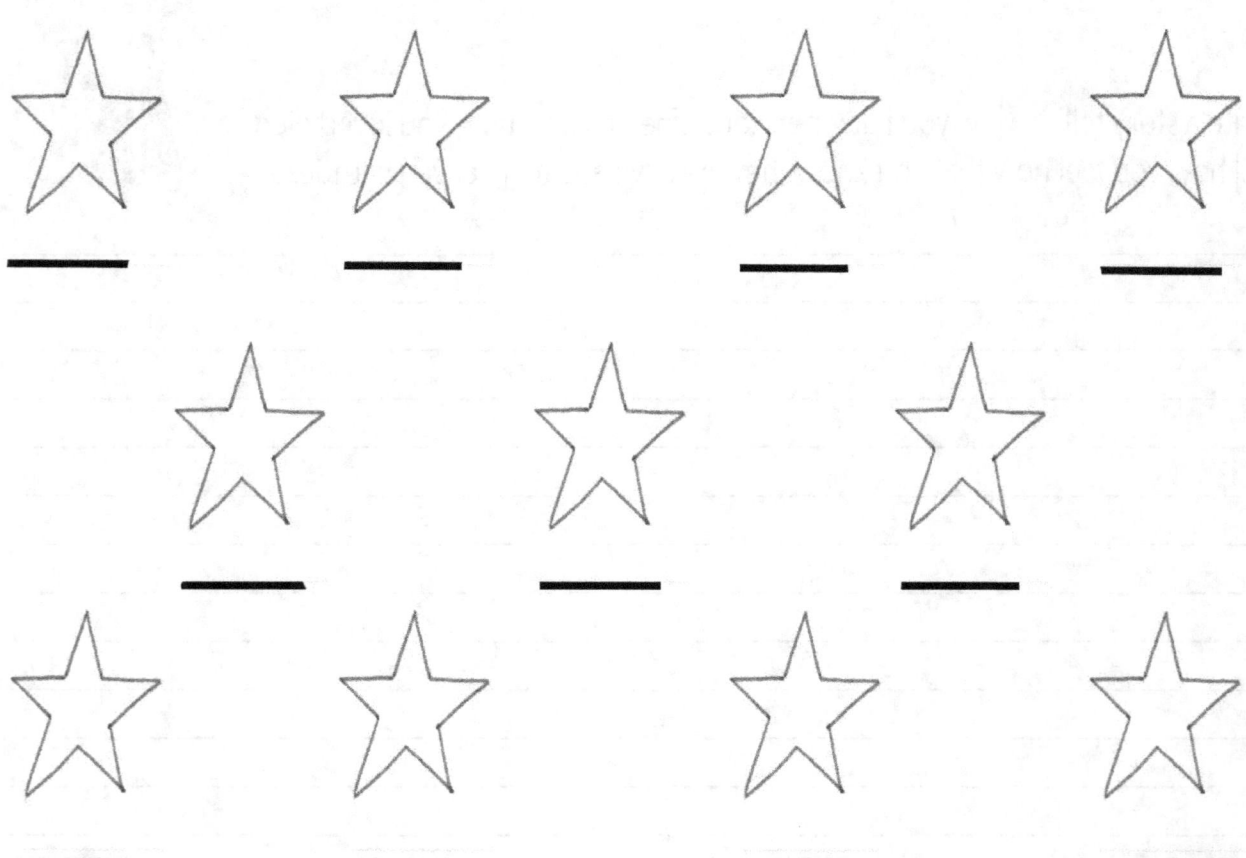

HOPES

we all hope for things...
          What do you hope for?

1._____
2._____
3._____
4._____

What can you do to make these hopes come true?

Hope #1_____
Hope #2_____
Hope #3_____
Hope #4_____

What are some good feelings that come with having hopes?

_____
_____
_____
_____
_____
_____

HOPES

Just as you have hopes for yourself, so do others have hopes for you. Sometimes these hopes are similar to the ones you have, and sometimes these hopes are different.

what do the following people hope for you?

Teacher: _____
_____

Parents: _____
_____

Friend: _____
_____

Grandparent: _____
_____

HOPES CONTINUED...

1. What do you think next year will be like?_____
_____

2. What are some of your hopes for next year? _____
_____

3. What do you think are Jesus' hopes for you? _____
_____

4. You are like a tree. What things do you need to help you grow?
Using the tree, write in the spaces for each word.

HOPE

Each letter of the word HOPE, write words that begin with that letter.

H_____
_____
O_____
_____
P_____
_____
E_____
_____

Think of some of the people who were not accepted in Jesus' day. Who were they?

_____
_____
_____
_____

Who are some of the people in your school, and in the world who are not accepted today? Why?

_____
_____
_____
_____

Are there people who do not accept you?

_____
_____
_____
_____

What feelings does a person have when he/she is rejected?

_____
_____
_____
_____

Your family is special to you. Jesus wants your family to be happy.

Think about what you can do to make your family happy.
Fill this out and put it on your fridge.

Things I willl try to do for my family.

MONDAY: _____
_____

TUESDAY: _____
_____

WEDNESDAY: _____
_____

THURSDAY: _____
_____

FRIDAY: _____
_____

SATURDAY: _____
_____

SUNDAY: _____
_____

There are many signs that we use to symbolize PEACE.

Draw the symbol you know, and create a new one.

Use the letters in the word PEACE to make a word list of PEACE words.

P_____

e_____

a_____

c_____

e_____

If people from different parts of the world, and of different religons got together in friendship. to build a house of God, what would you see?

Draw a picture of what it would look like.

TRAVEL

We can't travel around the world the way Paul did, but we can still give Jesus to others:
At home, in the school yard, on the street when we play.

How can we do this? Draw an example in the shapes.

At home...

In the school yard..

On the street...

 # JESUS IS LIKE THE SUN

When the sun is shining, everything grows. When the sun is shining everyone is happy. When the sun is shining, everything is bright and cheerful. When we let Jesus into our life, we feel happy. When Jesus shines his spirit into our life, we feel happy. When Jesus shines in our spirit by the way we act toward others, we grow into better people.

Make a picture of how you think you look when you let Jesus into your life.

RELIGIONS *of the* WORLD

Here are some beliefs of other Religions. Comment on what you think is good about their way of thinking.

HINDUISM: Cannot eat meat because animals are sacred. All life is sacred.

_____

BUDDHISM: Avoid being selfish and help others.

_____

TAOISM: They get close to nature and respect what it says.

_____

JUDAISM: To be happy, you must obey the law of God.

_____

ISLAM: To get to heaven, you must be charitable.

_____

GOD'S GIFT

READ CORINTHIANS   Ch. 3:1-13

Answer these questions

1. What are the gifts that Paul is speaking of?

_____

_____

2. What does Paul say is the greatest gift?

_____

_____

3 What are some of the qualities of this gift?

_____

_____

4 Do you think the people of Corinth were open to these gifts God offered?

_____

_____

5. Are you and your friends open to this gift? How?

_____

_____

Color Jesus

Jesus is alive in all of us. He wants us to be our best so that others can see him in us. Jesus is in our parents, teachers, and friends. We see Jesus in them when they do good things for others.

We see Jesus in our parents when they do things that keep us healthy and safe.

We see Jesus in our teachers when they are caring and help us learn.

We see Jesus in our friends when they say nice things to us, share with us, and play with us.

Tell us when you have seen Jesus in what others have done.

Parents: _____

_____

Teachers: _____

_____

Friends: _____

_____

What should I do?

Write what you would do

A friend falls and hurts an ankle.

_____
_____
_____
_____

A new student feels left out.

_____
_____
_____
_____

Some students are teasing someone in your class.

_____
_____
_____
_____

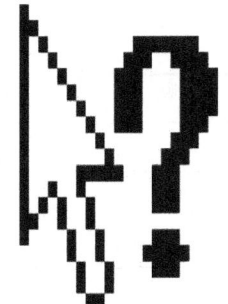

You see someone stealing.

_____
_____
_____
_____

MARY

Mary took care of Jesus and Joseph until they died. She took care of her friends and relatives too. Mary was a very caring person. She alwas helped out even when she was tired or not feeling well.

Write down what kinds of things Mary did for Jesus, Joseph, Elizabeth and John.

_____

_____

_____

_____

_____

_____

_____

_____

_____

_____

_____

_____

WORD SHAPES...

Think of a shape. Write a message around it.

Examples

Draw inside the box

*Cut it out after, and give it to someone in the class

PICTURE SHAPES...

Pick a shape. Write a message inside it. Read your message to the class.

Example

When the sun is out everything is bright. When we play in the sunlight we have fun. God made the sun to help things grow. Jesus asks us to be like him. He asks us to be nice to each other and help anyone who needs it. When we act this way we are like Jesus. We are like the sun, making everything shine. Alleluia!

Draw inside the box

FEELING GOOD

There are many things that prevent us from accepting love from others, and the love of Jesus. This causes us to be like a prisoner to our bad feelings and thoughts.

#1. Write down all the bad feelings and emotions that keeps us prisoners.

#2. This picture shows bolts of lightening that breaks the bars that frees us from prison.
On each bolt, write a good feeling or emotion that makes us free.

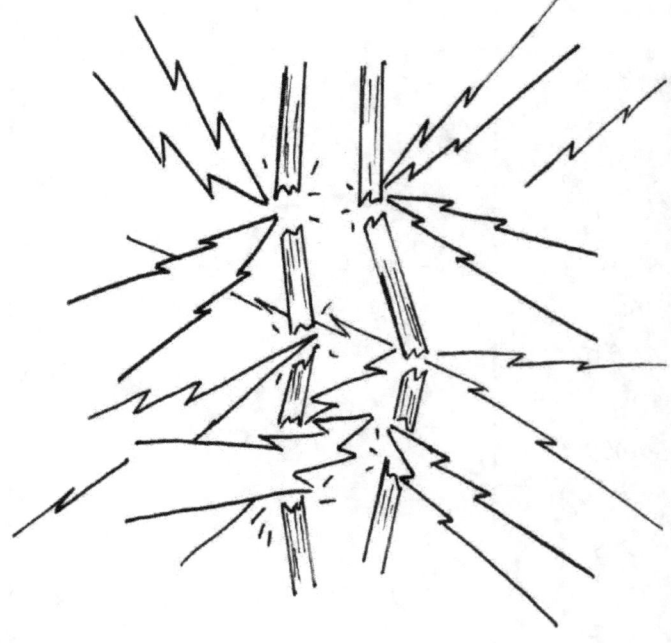

CARING PEOPLE

Think of some of the people who care about you. Write a short story below, telling how they helped you.

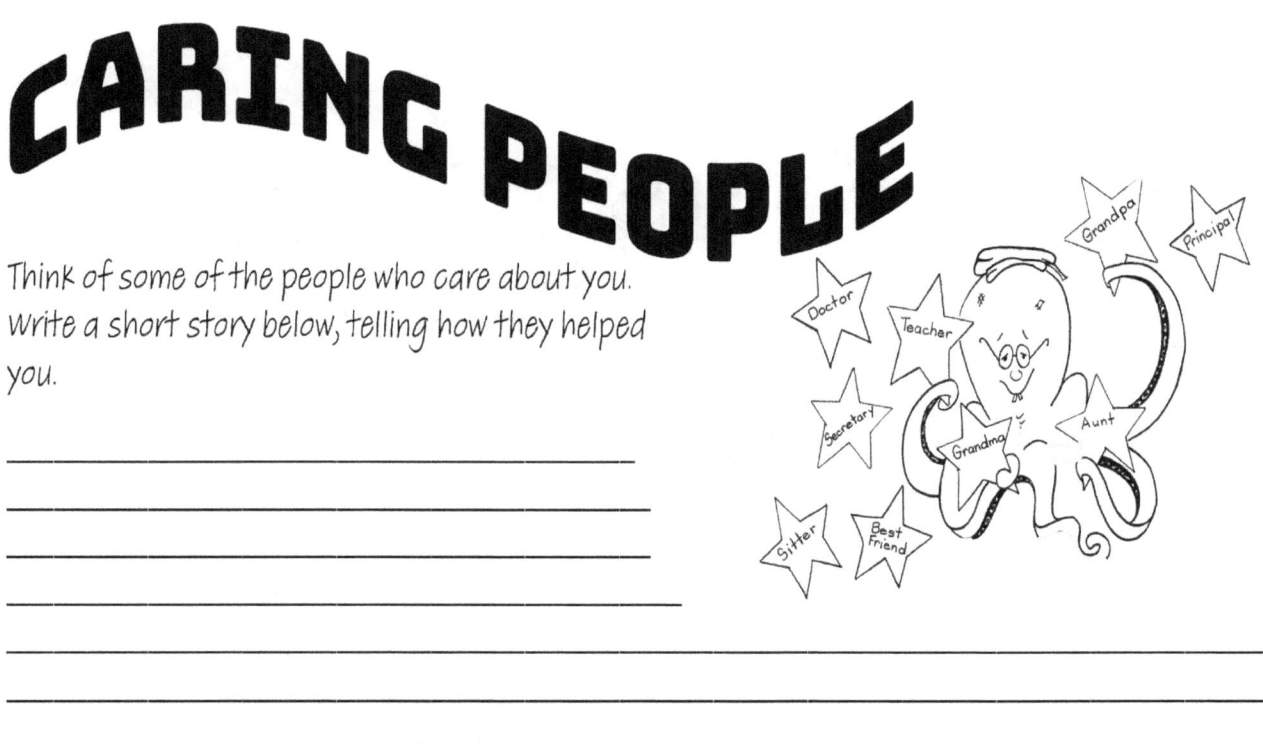

_____

_____

_____

_____

_____

_____

_____

Draw a picture of your teacher helping you.

BECOME A FORGIVING PERSON

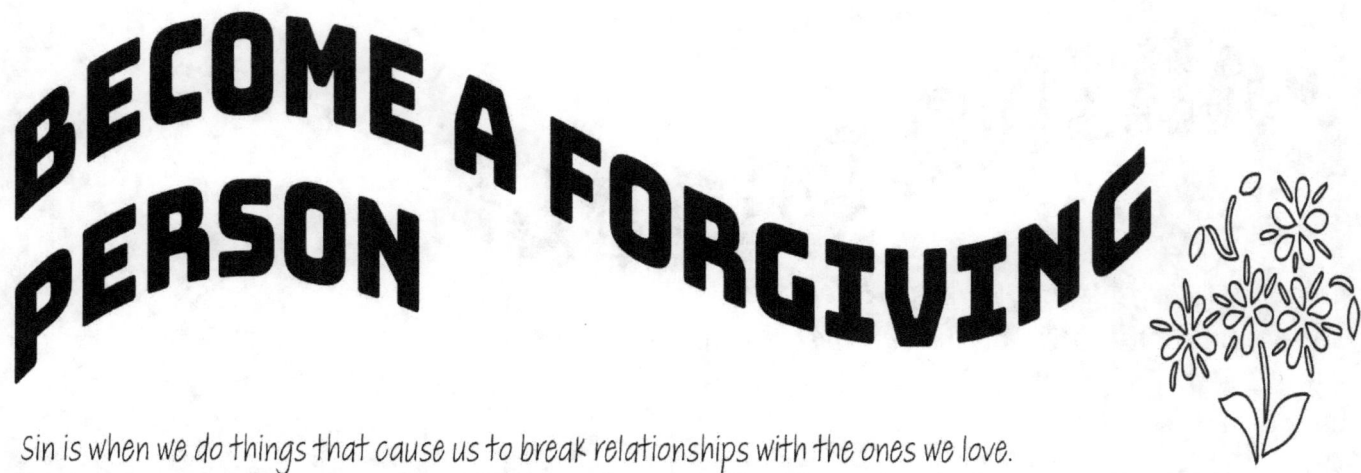

Sin is when we do things that cause us to break relationships with the ones we love.
We sin when we hurt, or destroy something that is good.

In the following 4 areas in your life, tell how you can improve your relationship.

GOD	SELF	OTHERS	NATURE

An
Invitation
To My
Party !

Make an invitation inviting some friends to your party. This is a party where you can get to know your friends better. It will be a special celebration.

Tell your Friends what they will be doing when they come to your party. .

Draw a picture on the front
once its cut out.

Your invited,

_____
_____
_____
_____
_____
_____
_____
_____
_____

From, _____

Everyone has something special to give us.

We can learn how special each person is by spending our time with each one of them.

Fill in the blanks

Happy
Cross
Died
Help
Pray
Heaven
God
Mary
Love
Life

1. Jesus was afraid, so He went into the garden to _____.
2. Jesus asked his Father for _____.
3. Jesus knew that he had to do what his _____ wanted.
4. Jesus knew that one day He would be with his Father in _____.
5. Jesus knew he would be _____ with his Father in Heaven
6. Jesus _____ on the cross for you.

Heaven is a wonderful place where God will love us and take care of us forever.

Make a picture of what you think Heaven is like. Put 5 things in your picture that you want to be with you in Heaven.

Unscramble the words and answer the questions

delcans   1. It is lit during Mass, and makes the church bright.

_____

scros   2. It is on the altar, and reminds us of Jesus' love.

_____

drbea   3. Father give us this to remember God's love and have Jesus in us.

_____

tpsrei   4. This person says Mass.

_____

fofteyr   5. This is when we bring up our Gifts.

_____

gnso   6. We sing this in church.

_____

Make up 3 words for the class to unscramble

1. _____ 2. _____ 3. _____